Hold on to Uranus and prepare for a coloring adventure that is out of this world! Grab your coloring supplies and get Cat Butts In Space (The Feline Frontier) ready for liftoff!

If you enjoy this book and would like to share it with others, please leave a review!

To keep up with the latest, follow @valbrains & @catbuttcoloring on instagram.

Cover Photo: Hamish Dowson on Unsplash

#icoloredcatbutts   #catbuttcoloringbook   @catbuttcoloring

CAT BUTTS IN SPACE

THE FELINE FRONTIER

A COLORING BOOK

© VALBRAINS 2019

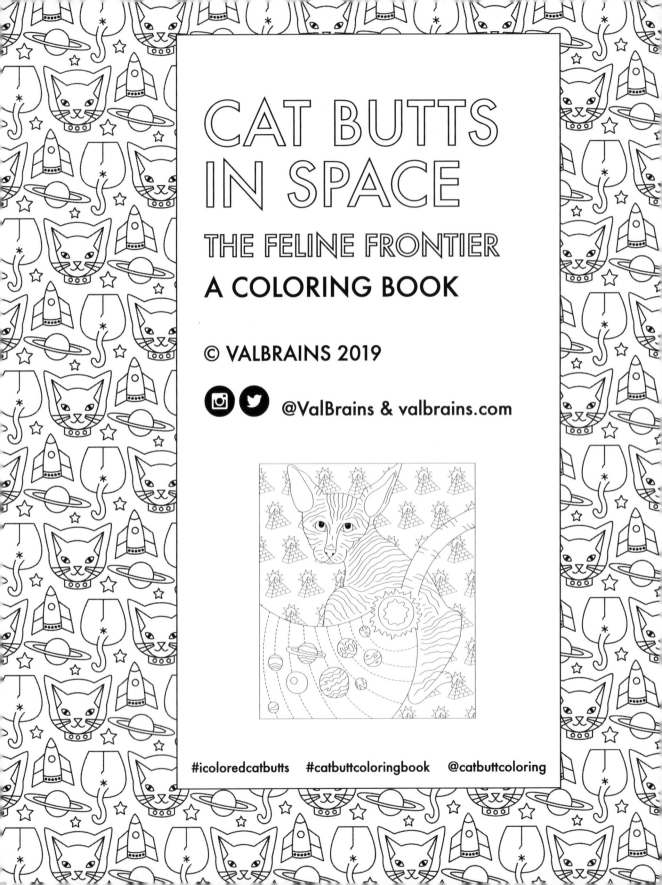 @ValBrains & valbrains.com

ZERO CAVITY

fold down

Colored by:

To:

fold up

MAGICAL MEOWNIVERSE

fold down

To:
Colored by:

fold up

READY FOR LIFTOFF!

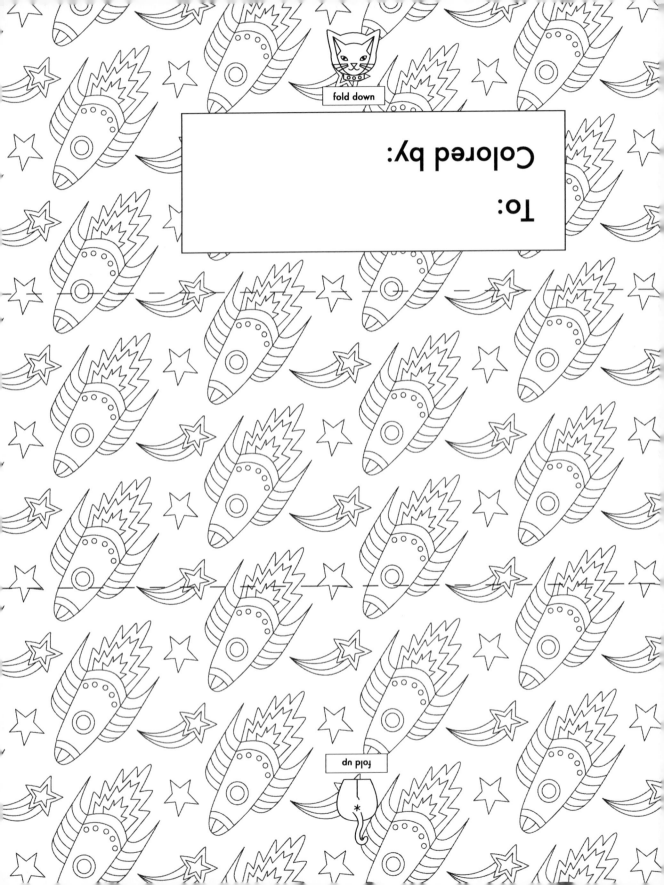

fold down

To:

Colored by:

fold up

CONNECT - THE - BUTTS

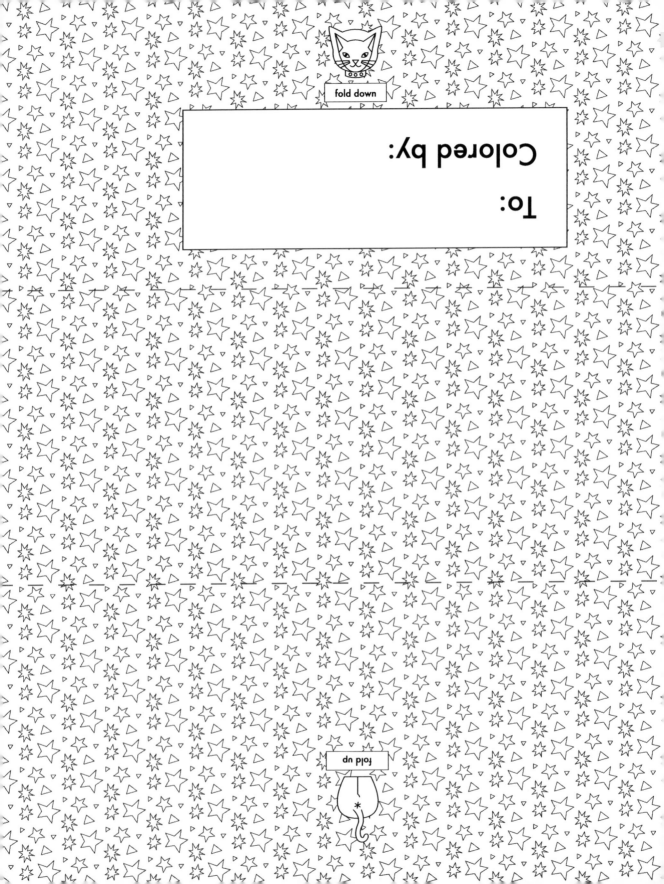

fold down

To:

Colored by:

fold up

ONE GIANT LEAP FOR BUTTKIND

fold down

To:

Colored by:

fold up

RECTAL RUNWAY

fold down

To:

Colored by:

fold up

I CAN SEE URANUS!

fold down

To:

Colored by:

fold up

SPACE CATELLITE

fold down

To:

Colored by:

fold up

BUM ME UP!

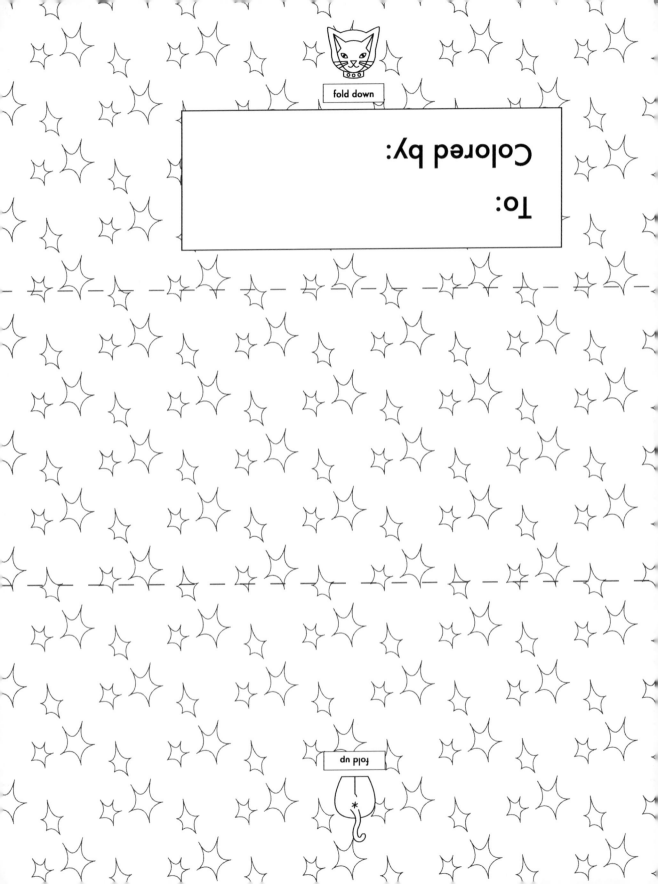

fold down

To:

Colored by:

fold up

COMMANDER CAT BUTT

fold down

To:
Colored by:

fold up

ALIEN ENCOUNTER

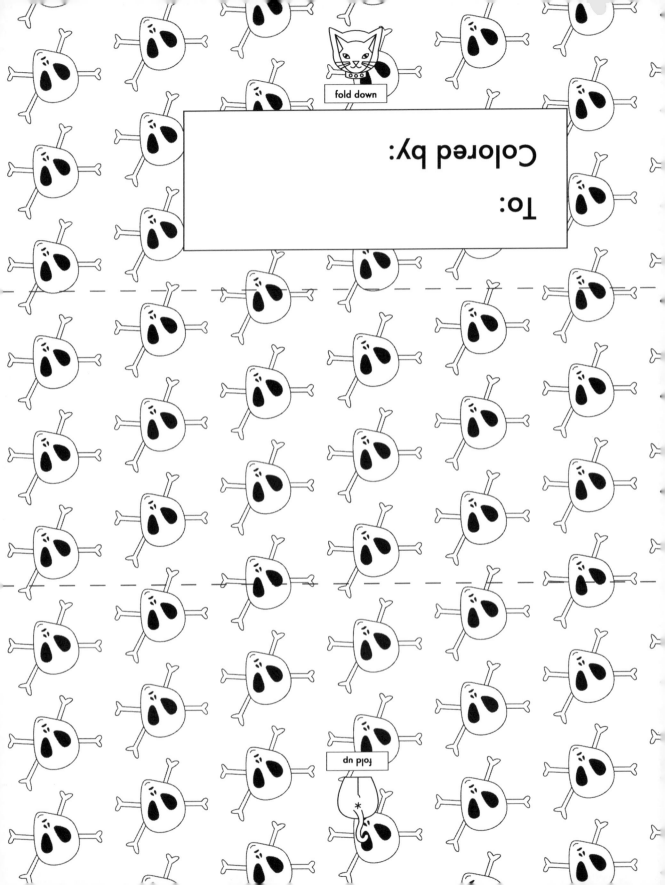

fold down

To:

Colored by:

fold up

ASTROCATS

fold down

To:

Colored by:

fold up

LASER BUMS

fold down

Colored by:

To:

fold up

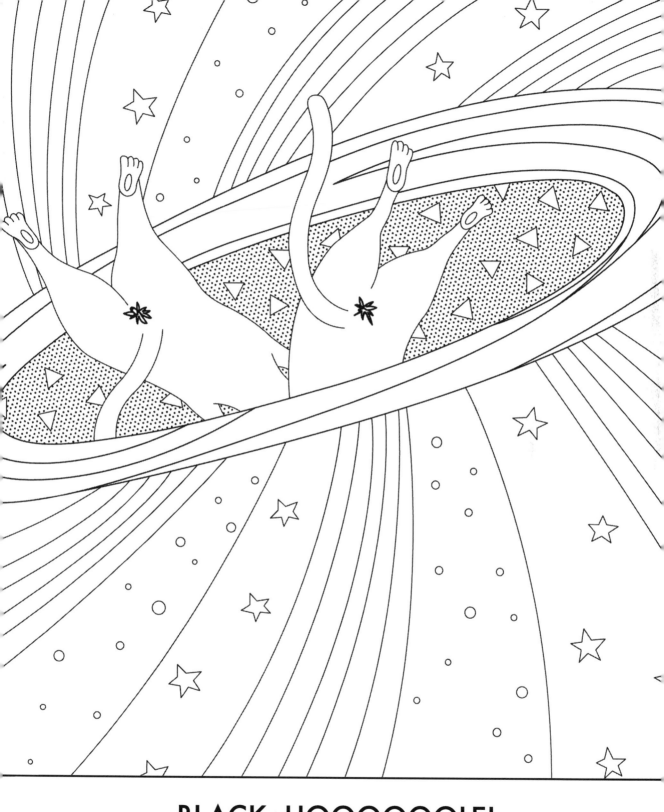

BLACK HOOOOOOLE!

fold down

To:

Colored by:

fold up

CELEBRATED CATSMONAUT

fold down

To:

Colored by:

fold up

FLOATING IN ORBUTT

fold down

To:

Colored by:

fold up

HOLE - AR SYSTEM

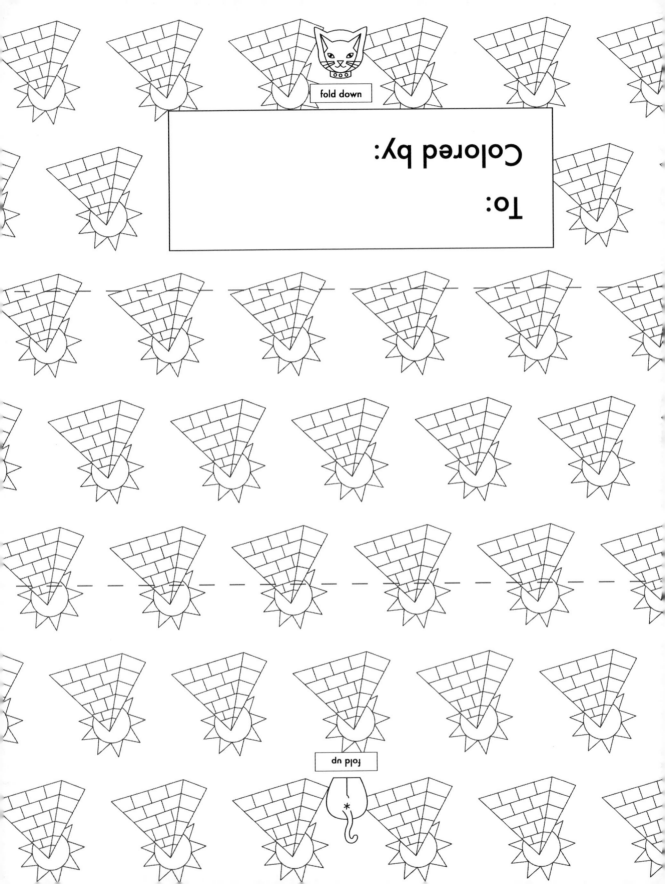

fold down

To:

Colored by:

fold up

FULL MOON

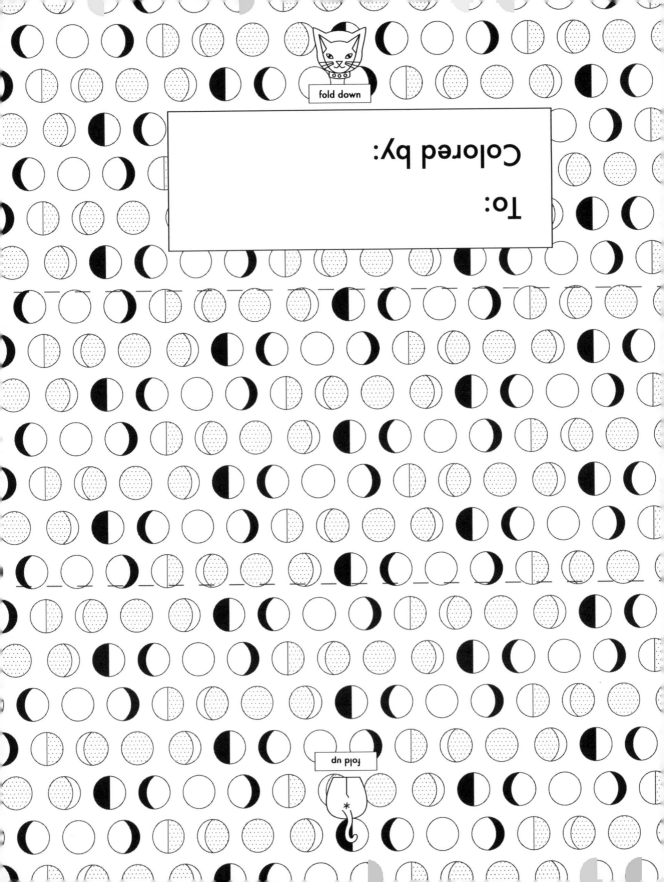

fold down

To:

Colored by:

fold up

RING AROUND URANUS!

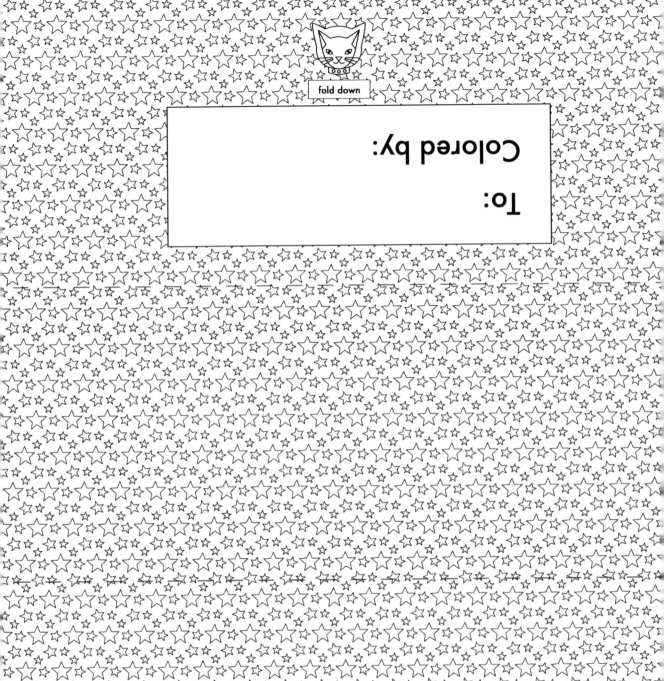

fold down

Colored by:

To:

fold up

PEW - PEW POWER!

fold down

To: Colored by:

fold up

A
CAT BUTTS IN SPACE
HAIKU

The Feline Frontier
Where no one has gone before
Color those Cat Butts!

Thank you for reading!

CAT BUTTS IN SPACE
THE FELINE FRONTIER
A COLORING BOOK

I appreciate your thoughtful and honest reviews!

If you would like to leave a review:

1. head to amazon.com
2. click "orders" at the top
3. then, "Write a product review."

⬇ Check out my other books! ⬇

Cat Butt Coloring Books:
The Cat Butt Coloring & Activity Book
Cat Butts In Space: The Feline Frontier
Cat Butt Birthday
Cat Butt Christmas
Cat Butt Hanukkah
Cat Butts In Love
Cat Butt Halloween
Cat Butt Or ... ?

more at valbrains.com! ➡

Other Funny Coloring & Gift Books:
The Tiger King Coloring & Activity Book
The Tanuki Coloring Book
The Butthole Coloring Book
The Best Dick Coloring Book
Where Is All The Toilet Paper?
Squirrel Nuts
Hexes for the Modern Age
Poop: A Coloring Book
Animal Poop: A Coloring Book
F*ck Flowers: A Swear Word Coloring Book
It Had To Be Poo: A Valentine's Coloring Book
The Ultimate Bro Coloring Book
Xmas Sharks: A Coloring Book

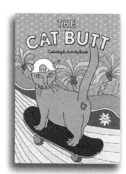

THE
CAT BUTT
Coloring & Activity Book

CAT BUTTS
IN SPACE
THE FELINE FRONTIER
A COLORING BOOK

CAT BUTT
BIRTHDAY!
A COLORING BOOK

CAT BUTT
CHRISTMAS!
A COLORING BOOK

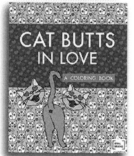

CAT BUTTS
IN LOVE
A COLORING BOOK

CAT BUTT
HALLOWEEN
A COLORING BOOK

CAT BUTT
OR ... ???
A COLORING BOOK

CAT BUTT
HANUKKAH
A COLORING BOOK

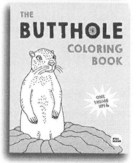

THE
BUTTHOLE
COLORING BOOK
ONE THUMB UP!

the tanuki
coloring book

THE
TIGER KING
COLORING & ACTIVITY BOOK
Homage? Parody?
YOU decide!

where is all the
TOILET PAPER?
A COLORING BOOK

SQUIRREL
NUTS
A COLORING BOOK

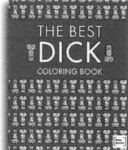

THE BEST
DICK
COLORING BOOK

XMAS
SHARKS!
A COLORING BOOK

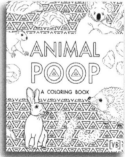

ANIMAL
POOP
A COLORING BOOK

IT HAD TO BE
POO
A VALENTINE'S COLORING BOOK

THE ULTIMATE
BRO
COLORING BOOK

F*CK
FLOWERS
A SWEAR WORD
ADULT COLORING BOOK
BY FLORA CUBBINGHAM

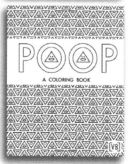

POOP
A COLORING BOOK

Printed in Great Britain
by Amazon